requiem

Books by Virginia Konchan

Vox Populi
Anatomical Gift
The End of Spectacle
The New Alphabets
That Tree Is Mine
Any God Will Do
Hallelujah Time
Bel Canto
Requiem

requiem
virginia konchan

Carnegie Mellon University Press
Pittsburgh 2025

Acknowledgments

Grateful acknowledgement is made to the editors of the following journals, in which these poems first appeared:

The Account: "Lamentation" and "Anemone"; *Action, Spectacle*: "Afterimage," "Intercession," "Childlessness," and "Optimism"; *Alaska Quarterly Review*: "L'Heure Bleu" and "Privacy"; *The Atlantic*: "Vigil"; *The Banyan Review*: "Solar Plexus"; *Bennington Review*: "Antithesis"; *The Café Review*: "Elegy" and "Convert"; *Cider Press Review*: "Palinode"; *The Common*: "Sonata," "Overture," "Antiphon," "Carpe Diem" and "Cogito"; *The Cortland Review*: "Doxology"; *The Gettysburg Review*: "Prelude" and "Human Resources"; *The Laurel Review*: "Midlife" and "Coda"; *The Missouri Review*: "Apostrophe," "Ecce Homo," "Miraculous," "Confessional" and "Apocalypse"; *New American Writing*: "Symbiosis," "Relic," and "Pilgrim"; *New Letters*: "Epistemology" and *"Mont-Blanc"*; *The New Yorker*: "Gloria Patri"; *Poem-a-Day*: "Ubi Sunt" and "Black Hole"; *The Rumpus*: "Parousiamania"; *Sixth Finch*: "Applicant"; *Southern Indiana Review*: "Sola Gratia"; *swamp pink*: "Valediction"; *THRUSH*: "Dear Victoria"; *The Walrus*: "Second Nature"

"Miraculous" appears in *The Best American Poetry 2025*.

Profound thanks to Gerald Costanzo, Cynthia Lamb, Connie Amoroso, and the wonderful team at Carnegie Mellon University Press for their support and care with the publication of this book, and the previous three collections I have had the honor of publishing with Carnegie Mellon. Jerry, I owe my existence as a poet to you. Thank you for the gifts of seeing and recognition, for shepherding my books into the world, and for the blessing of finding the perfect home with you, a firm foundation on which to grow my roots and wings. Thank you for being my first and best reader, for carrying me. I celebrate your visionary legacy and fierce dedication with all my heart.

Immense thanks to the Berkshire Taconic Community Foundation and the Amy Clampitt Fund committee for the support of a residency at the Amy Clampitt House in Lenox, Massachusetts, from July to December 2023. Thank you to my neighbors Emily Pulfer-Terino, Chris Himes, and Robin Getzen for holiday gatherings, friendship, and inviting me to teach at Miss Hall's School. To Paul Graubard, Requiem's first reader: thank you for inspiring my confidence in this book, and for your sublime art. To Karen, thank you for your magnificent painting, and presence.

Deepest gratitude to my family, friends and to early readers: Bruce Bond, Ama Codjoe, John Hennessy, Nathan McClain, Joshua Marie Wilkinson, Matthew Lippman, Chris Stroffolino, Cynthia Mitchell, Kathleen Rooney, Geoff Bouvier, Wyn Cooper, and Andrew Zawacki.

John Vincent, thank you for your discerning mind, buoyant heart, and listening ear. I wouldn't know how to weather storms without you. Chris Stasa, thank you for being my trusted witness, counselor, and confidante in the ways of spirit. Kathleen Rooney, you are friendship incarnate, an earth angel embodying brilliance, loyalty, and grace. Caitlyn Doyle: your essence is joy. Thank you for laughter, kinship, and for holding the faith with me in brighter futurities.

My largest debt of gratitude is to my mother, Theresa McNamara Konchan, who passed away on December 23, 2023. She blessed me with existence, language, and love. The anticipatory grief I felt when she entered hospice were what brought these poems about mourning into existence, but nothing could have prepared me to say goodbye. Mom, I am yours and you are mine, forever.

Book design by Anna Cappella

for the beloved departed

God is of no importance unless He is of supreme importance.

—Abraham Heschel

Contents

1.

2.

3.

1.

Matins

The philosopher sat shiva with his shadow,
knowing the truth was without and within.
The clay he was wouldn't take him there,
nor the flag rippling wildly in harsh wind.
Abraham waited, as did David and Joseph,
Moses, Hannah, Isaiah, Ruth, Jacob, Paul.
Each hour an unmet hunger, an ardent plea.
Each hour a pointillist dot on a map whose
design it would surely destroy them to see.
I read my child their favorite bedtime story,
happy ending memorized, again and again:
solemn dance between abandon and control
of a narrative they have not participated in
except as an inveterate reader of the world,
turning each page slowly, as if surprisingly.
I, too, will practice awe, bending at the knee.
Before we were orphans, we were innocent.
Before we were ornament, we were names
moving in a mouth, each syllable a victory.
Romantic love may not exist how I imagine:
miracle of the body catching up to the mind.
To deny oneself the garden is to deny home:
origin story abjured from a prehistoric time.
A vernal equinox draws near, sun above the
equator squaring the lengths of night and day.
Women, bloodshed, eye of newt, witchy hair—
narcotic undertow of the somnambulist moon
beckons to bright germination, spirit of play.
For every tragedy, a lo-fi postmodern sunset.
For every gold star, a rote round of applause.
If there is a beyond, it must be pure harmony:
praising in the morning, faithfulness at night,
a canticle of creation delighting in your laws.

Privacy

Call it what it is:
angel lost in my body,
torn down shrubbery
that once functioned
as a partition between
your house and mine.
There I go again,
chasing what I can
never have, what it was
never mine to be given.
The sky's conducting
the river like a maestro:
current electric as eel.
The small of my back
convulsing with pain
as I forage the sludge,
past skunk cabbages
and wrecked carcasses,
past my sullen petulance
and years of grave folly
now seen in high relief,
wrestling with language
as Jacob wrestled with
his heaven-sent guide—
to a field of flowering
vetch, where I pause
to drink in darkness.
Take this carapace,
take these vestments,
take what is derivative,
and give me in exchange
a cool draught of water
lifted from a deep well.

The soul, vestigial thing,
cries out sharply, as if
wounded or alarmed.
But no harm has come,
nor intended to come,
to this solitary figure
standing in the clearing
shaded by a lemon tree.
Here I am: shelter me.

Palinode

We are protagonists stuck in a Greek tragedy
wherein the chorus knows more than we do
yet refuses to share their insights or advice
through peripheral narration and dithyramb.
Professional critics of disinterested passion:
I don't want to blow up, I want to disappear.
I can't know my most intrinsic motivation,
but I think it is the dream of a unified field.
Units of pressure, power, energy, or force:
will the end come as a binomial equation,
a theorem, a philosophy, or a work of art?
Birth order theory, quantum gravity theory,
prevailing wisdom and hypocrisy of the day:
it's not that I don't trust you. I trust me more,
a baseline introvert with prosocial tendencies.
With God, all things are possible, such as God.
Including parables, apologias, cautionary tales
and their denouements, in ontogenetic primacy.
Atoms, electrons, photons, quarks, dark matter:
the degradation of the actual has a long history.
Once again confounding annuals and perennials,
I have the desire to have the desire to wring your
supraspinatus muscle of all tension and fatigue.
Among the heterogeneity in all the cases I see,
yours alone intrigues me: ancient in your fear,
you testify to transcendence, black tabernacle
housing the bling of real presence, in eternity.

Pastorale

Stalked by paparazzi of my own making
in a hyperlinked garden of forking paths,
I'm chain mail in search of an addressee.
Is this mic even on? I want to be honest,
but I see the wires. Serenity now, I say
to my alter ego, my father's incipient
dementia, my mother's brain tumor.
Am I serious? Hell yes I'm serious.
Serious as a heart attack, or a Jew.
In a room of malignant narcissists,
I am the engraved daguerreotype,
asking: what would Diogenes do?
There's no pill nor product left:
I cordon myself off, to grieve.
I need a strong French cheese,
stern advice, a retirement plan
from all the helping industries.
The security camera's footage
will reveal my sketch goodbye
from the elaborate production:
plain clothes private detective
striving for brand consistency
across hundreds of platforms,
the long European diseases
of alienation and solipsism
vanishing, like the shore
at high tide, from the sea.

War Horse

In the dream called war,
they called me by name.
After that, I was owned.
If not my destiny, whose?
Mother earth, father sky:
the heart wants what it wants.
Disinterested in human drama,
a motive written before time
on the soul, in superscript.
So I put on the blinders:
I allowed for saddle,
bridle, halters, reins.
Saw many men die.
Was the body in pain.
What do we remember
when we remember:
disfluency, ache?
Shadow puppets
dancing on a wall?
He convinced me:
it was all so private.
Life is complicated,
more so when trying
to live, which I wasn't,
made and spurred by a
maker on tenterhooks.
Intellectual traditions,
the history of ideas:
snakes in the grass.
O, the desecration.
He healed me before
those who broke me.
My god, my god,
my body returned—
ransom paid, at last.

Ecce Homo

The house where Nietzsche declared God
dead in Sils Maria, Switzerland is 18th c.
white stucco, with blue wooden shutters
and a sloping gable roof made of slate:
The Gay Science, originally translated
as *The Joyful Wisdom*, extols saying
yes to life, extrapolation from the sun.
Will the void forever be formless, spun:
the dramatic orchestration of subjectivity
unveiled to the sound of lapping waters?
So what if the philosophers are dreaming,
some with emptied faces, without gaze?
I admire the Etruscan art displayed at
the Met: wall frescos and terracotta
portraits discovered in tombs in Caere.
Funerary, urban, sacred are the themes.
O requisite partiality, O vexing finitude.
I offer you the shade of a canopied tree,
a humble heart, a vision of true sanctity.
Promise Keeper, Miracle Worker, Son
of Man with nowhere to lay your head:
outside the grinding maw of capital is
your voice, recoiling through centuries:
quiet and insistent as needle and thread.

Apostrophe

My husband didn't understand prayer.
He said people who pray are deranged.
Who do they think they're talking to?
Even with Bluetooth technology,
do they not know how ridiculous
they look, directing words to the sky?
Truth requires a suspension of belief,
I said. Science is only half the story.
You've taken ecstasy: you know
what it is to transcend the flimsy
bounds of body, space, and time.
O millennials. O anthropodicy.
Information underrepresents us:
bootleg liquor down the drain.
Do you remember the first night
we met, I asked, when we both
became addicted to that which
would never return, the stain?
Imagine singing a new song.
Imagine asking and receiving,
a surge of animated presence,
hoodwinked stars lighting up
the brazen, incandescent sky.
The opposite of a flat, literal,
unambiguous screen is God.
The opposite of a simulation
is a stimulation of the soul.
O alphanumeric characters.
O foothills of Appalachia.
That in your veins red life
might stream again, and I
be personified once more.

Second Nature

The moment I embrace, I'm told,
my Buddha nature is the moment
the light shines in. The moment
I allow the Holy Spirit to course
through me is when I'm healed.
What about my flower nature?
Chrysanthemum, peony, rose?
I've one that was run over with
a lawn mower, then a truck,
then a stampede of children,
before dying of pesticide
exposure, then drought.
Every year it comes back.
Every year it shakes its
lioness head and roars.
I'm of the nature of one
who, when suffering and
asked how I'm doing, say
no complaints through
a jaw clenched by grief.
What is my nature then?
That of a springboard,
turnstile, anvil, plank?
We see but darkly now
but will one day see
face to face, vis-à-vis
our being, undefiled:
a window cleared of
grime, Irish ivy or
another creeping
plant surrounding
the wood frame, as
branches do a vine.

L'Heure Bleue

Be drunk always, azure, azure, azure,
psychic life and origin of all vesture,
blue mandorla, Venus' vesica piscus:
jouissance and puissance, pharmakon.

Our bodies are 60% water: the heart
and brain, 73%, and the earth, 71%.
Blue-veined breast, rind, moon.
You are not the warmest color,

blue, nor hour, but you sedate the
emotionally disturbed in clinics
and carnivals: Aztecs smeared
the chests of their victims with

blue paint at the lowing altar.
The royal blue throat chakra is
associated with communication,
honesty, empathy, and calming

energy: the indigo ink of Mary,
indignant, as indigo is a cheap,
slave labor crop, called devil's
dye. Blue depression glass was

manufactured in the Ohio River Valley
during the war years of 20th century
America, in shades of cobalt,
delphite, and ultramarine.

Latin: *ultramarinus*, "beyond
the sea," made by grinding lapis
lazuli into a powder imported into
Europe from Afghanistan mines by

Italian traders in the 14th century.
The color of the Virgin's robes
in Renaissance paintings, it had
to be made holy by the wicked

logic that renders the expensive
sacred, symbolizing her humility.
The third primary color, after red
and yellow, it's opposite to orange

on color theory's prismatic wheel,
stigmatized by value, chroma, hue:
I can almost taste the burst of blue-
berries from the orchards of youth

breaking on the palate of tongue.
Blue, personified, loves you when
you're lonely, as does the oceanic
gaze of my father, relieving the sky

of religious connotations: alchemical
mediatrix, whirling dervish of flame.
The soul of Anima Mundi is maya.
Past monomania, hypomania, shock,

and grief to the blunt blue of pain,
the first color seen in the aura upon
awakening from a crushing migraine
to discover your Sapphire gin gone.

The spectrum of light emitted by
over 200,000 galaxies is turquoise:
the hottest stars radiate coolness.
Fifteen days after we are hatched,

we can discriminate between colors:
robin's egg, baby, slate, blue-green.
Cold-blooded snakes, blue-blooded
queens: lakes, estuaries, tributaries,

universal color of democratic liberty,
the other half of the American flag,
representing vigilance, perseverance,
and justice. Hungry ghosts, surgical

masks, mouths deprived of oxygen,
unable to breathe: we're not fish.
Krishna blue, immersive baptism
in the sultry scat of "Mojo Working,"

"I'd Rather Go Blind," *A Love Supreme.*
Sing the blues, servant of sadness, in
your powder, pastel blue bouffant cap
and laboratory coat, as you recede and

advance, subtractive and additive.
In astrophysics, blueshifting occurs
when the heavens move toward our
viewpoint on earth in the Book Of

Numbers, ribboning out to speak
to the Israelites and to them say:
"Throughout generations to come,
go make blue cords on the tassels

of your garments." Someday I shall
tell of your mysterious birth, silence
crossed by vowels, nouns, and angels,
delirium tremens of sacral sublimity.

Passion, aggression, spiritual possession:
O Omega, O hemophiliac chromophile.
Small blue flower with a yellow center
growing abundantly in the countryside,

you are a mirage, image, representation:
I feel your foot tapping like a phantom
on the floor. Tendril of clematis, cling
to the vine: be thou my miracle, whole.

Confessional

Most biographies of women read
like tragedy, even if inadvertently.
This one didn't have birth control.
That one also didn't, and, further,
lost everyone she loved in a freak
accident or due to natural causes.
Hysteria: Greek for "of the womb,"
which wanders inasmuch as mind.
I hark to the wise elders' counsel:
break a sweat every day. Climb a
hill every day. Call your mother.
Yet still, I soften the blow of an
opinion with a carefully curated
emoji, seek approval from others,
pay fealty to illusions of mastery.
Aspiring to creation or holiness
does not require chronic illness.
Work all your life to buy time to
do nothing is not an ideal creed.
Today, I bought a marzipan cake,
caught a draught of water and air,
admired the moody sky, a peony.
I did not starve myself, nor beg
for anything, nor perform any
rite of manufactured contrition.
Instead of being late, I never came.
Life is deadly serious, because death,
industrial violence of a shrieking train.
I walk in my house with a perfect heart,
unshattered: skin like porcelain or glass.
I acknowledge my maker's sovereignty.
I broker meanness without being mean.
This is the day I solve the problem of
finitude, the day I finally come clean.

Ubi Sunt

Where are the good ones:
the beautiful, strong, and
virtuous figures of yore?
Probably where the moon is,
hung aloft in effulgent skies:
eating nails for breakfast,
dying in childbirth, then
resurrecting to give it all
away, cyclically, once more.
I don't want to be the moon,
I said to Dick on the casting
couch: I want to be a flower
no one can touch without dying
of hope of touching it again.
Something rare and exotic:
throaty stamen, purple pistil.
Something that just stands
on the stage and screams.
Alas, that role is taken,
said Dick, by Suzanne.
Figures, I said. How
about the wild river,
he suggested, kindly.
Or a creek, brook,
rivulet, rill, stream?
But where do I empty,
I asked, before agreeing:
in an ocean, sea, or lake,
or do I just flow into the
ground, a dried-up shrew?
That's between you and your
character to decide, he said.
The river, you mean, I said.
Yes, he said. For god's sake,
you're a woman. Just be you.

Sola Gratia

I was good when it was difficult
to be good. Instead of whining
or shirking my responsibilities,
I showed up for life, teeth bared.
This is something nearly everyone
does. Long-suffering, not quitting,
doesn't make me special or good.
My 6th grade English teacher, in
searching for something positive
to share with my mother during
parent-teacher conferences, said,
after struggling for a while, that
I was "resourceful." My mother
clung to that word as if she had
been told I was the prize pupil,
marshalled it in times of duress,
reminding me how resourceful
I was, or could be: how, when
out of money I could beg for it.
How when my pen dried of ink,
I could use my own blood. I did.
This, too, didn't make me good.
What made me good was my
insistence on concordance.
How like a woman to agree.
Look at the world, only at one
when asleep, eyes sealed shut.
Look at all those land parcels,
already settled by feral birds.
You can price it. You can put
a stake in it, saying "For sale."
But it will never be yours, not
truly. What makes something

yours is what you sacrificed
to obtain it. How like a life,
to be unworthy of sacrifice.
How like a god, to be free.

Dear Victoria

I've so often been called your name,
despite Victoria not being my name,
that I'm starting to confuse the two.
You: alter ego, doppelgänger, muse.

I picture you in a brothel. I picture you
in an art museum. I picture you saying
no to the yes man when he comes to call,
flouncing your purple tulle, or crinoline.

Victoria: a steady glucose drip in veins,
an apostate kneeling, a rose with thorns.
What my mother would have wished for
me, had she been well enough to wish.

I attract Geminis, but don't get them,
Victoria: it's part of my karmic wheel.
Could you offer some insight on that
matter, or any other matter, queen?

I could remove you forcibly from me,
purblind feline, but why rid myself
of the one good thing about me:
people confusing me with you?

When names and significations end,
I will be sitting near a dumpster on
some unfortunate street in America,
far away from the maddening crowd.

I will be silently chanting Victoria:
the undergarment to my destiny,
stock joke in a random exchange,
piercing blade in a cutthroat brawl.

African violet, Whitmanian lilac:
do you prefer cologne to perfume?
Half-witted half-woman, half-man:
you see, it's you who need me now.

Epistemology

So much I can't know:
my cat, is she staring at
or through the window?
Of what does she dream
when she chatters nonsense
to the birds, are her sounds
a promise or a threat, and
does she humor me, or I her
when I murmur sweet nothings
into the upturned conch of her ear—
a pale pink, miniature, roving satellite?
My little gladiola, golden harp, reason
for continuance, hothouse English pea:
if life would be so kind, I would
serve you even better after dearth,
pardon me, death. Je m'excuse,
sickle cell anemia, Alzheimer's,
measles, shingles, leprosy, gout:
ours was an overnight affair.
Psalmist returned to singing,
before whom nations kneel:
it's only when time is spent
that I value it, baroque pearl.
It's only then, at world's end,
on some enchanted evening
beneath empyrean skies
that I know I'll never die,
and that only love is real.

Parousiamania

Why would I expect a tired employee,
overworked, uninsured, and underpaid,
to devise a surefire exit plan from hell?
That would be akin to thinking one can
learn about men by watching them shave:
scribbles on the margins of an evangelical
tract handed out near the entrance for free.
Have I accepted Jesus Christ as my Lord
and Savior? Amen. But enough about me.
When bored, I make a list of things I want,
like a car that runs or jeans that actually fit.
I am the volcano's lip, a milk tooth teething,
Kodak moment ruined by campground wolves:
annual pilgrimage to a multinational superstore
aborted, midmission, upon discovery of mind.
Animals do not leave documents. Ghosts
do not speak to other ghosts, or engage in
parallel, constructive, or cooperative play.
I need a priest to perform the dying rites
of Divine Unction in aisle 29, beside
a pyramid of alabaster toilet paper.
When I rouse myself back to life,
I'll weigh the distance between
perspectival and hourly shifts
before commandeering this
shopping cart the way people
are raptured: up, up, and away.

Mont-Blanc

The architecture of surveillance is clear,
watching me watch myself pitch forward
into space, knocking into objects, almost
unable to breathe. I lived in a city where,
on December 6, 1917, a Norwegian vessel,
SS *Imo*, collided with a French cargo ship,
SS *Mont-Blanc* in the Narrows, a strait
connecting the Atlantic harbor to the basin,
thus releasing 2.9 kilotons of trinitrotoluene:
the largest human-made explosion to date,
it killed almost 2,000 people instantly and
wounded another 9,000 who were within
a half-mile radius of the blast. A shock
wave traveling at 23 times the speed of
sound snapped trees, bent iron rails, and
wrecked buildings; a pyrocumulus cloud
rose 12,000 feet in the air; and a tsunami,
formed by water surging in to fill the void
created when the harbor floor was exposed
carried what was left of the ships to shore,
and wiped out a surrounding community.
Halifax is haunted, said a local resident,
by all the souls displaced instantaneously
when the *Imo* tried to pass *Mont-Blanc* on
her starboard side, not port to port—the left.
Despite several blows of the captains' signal
whistles to indicate who had the right of way,
engines cut, the momentum was yet too strong,
and the *Imo*'s prow struck *Mont-Blanc*'s hold,
breaking open barrels of benzol, which ignited.
The panicked crew immediately abandoned ship,
and shouted from their two lifeboats to the other
nearby vessels, trying to warn them of the blast,

but no one could hear them over the commotion,
and even if they could, they were speaking French.
Navire de saut, I imagine they yelled: *dépêche-toi.*
It's a disaster to be lost in translation, they must
have felt, crying out *Elle va exploser . . . elle va.*

Afterimage

Past the dive bar. Past the nightclubs.
Past the cobblestone, piss-soaked streets.
Past the smokestack, windmill, Boeing jet.
Past the oxygenated arboretum, the train
and its steel tracks hauling cargo, freight.
Past paranoia, scopophilia: past avalanche,
cavalcade, honeysuckle's ambrosial balm.
Past the time-lapse photo of a falling star,
new embryo, a germinating cosmos seed:
past the soul's habits, attitudes, postures,
living testament to the weight of history.
Past where language ends and god begins.
What is wealth but adding zeroes to a sum?
Past eyeballing the latest wares and gadgets
brokering satisfied contentment, for a spell:
beyond bliss of surfeit, elemental reverie.
Past the production of knowledgeability
to the dim corridor of communicability.
Past the hem of Christ's robe, to the idea
of infinity. Past dataism, quantification,
disembodied cerebration, to celebration.
Past the serrated edge of angelic wings.
Past wherever you happen to suddenly
be, entangled like a caterwauling cat
in the late twilight of the humanities,
to an open field studded with violets
declaring grief and joy contrapuntal.
Past recitation, scrambling for keys.
After metaphors of light, comes light—
human life the fault line, vindication
of what it means to breath, to breathe.

Miraculous

Outside, the air is perfume sweet,
the sky suffused in motherly hues.
A rich tapestry called past tense
unfolds, like a scroll, before me:
the future beckons, then leaves.
But what's truly amazing is this:
I step into traffic and it swerves.
I drink poison and vomit it out.
I encounter people who desire
to kill me with their bare hands,
and several have tried, only to
find their weapons shattered,
their ways scattered and lost.
Blessed, the poor and lowly:
blessed are they who mourn.
Tell a dream, lose a reader, but
every day, I swear, I am reborn.
Every day I meet with an angel.
Some minister to me, tenderly:
others clean and dress my wounds.
Some make it rain, mysteriously:
a very few pierce me through
my heart with arrows made of
alabaster marble and pure gold.
You might think I'm freaking,
but I'm wide awake, like Job.
You may think I'm joking, but
I'm not prone to joke anymore.
Thy rod and staff, they comfort:
I abide, and in abiding, forbear.
What if grace holds me together?
What if heaven is what earth is for?

Vigil

Overwatered the fire lilies.
Underwatered the aloe.
Prayed to the sun god
to dispel my gloom.
Bought perlite and peat moss.
Made cuttings out of dahlia,
aster, gardenia, begonia, rose.
Charged crystals in the moon.
Claimed knowledge panels.
Accessed several past lives.
Testified to my greenery
of vistas yet unknown.
Drank vinegar.
Ate seldomly.
Consulted no one
except those the
spirit guides approved.
Was stringent, exacting.
Practiced loving action.
Rode my bike through
abandoned streets that
led to stately mansions
with automated sprinklers
misting trees from Brazil.
Spoke candidly in private:
was speechless in public.
A return to civilian life
without halo or word.
Formed energy grids.
Awoke Kundalini.
Sought true friends,
not those whom ego
or mere habit serves.

All this time my mother
lay dying in hospice, alone.
I held her paper-thin hand.
Rubbed her feet with oils.
Kissed her ancient forehead.
Embraced her body of bone.

Valediction

Today is all we have. Today was also all we had
yesterday, and will be all we have yet tomorrow.
How are we supposed to sleep at night, save for
the utter exhaustion of our biodegradable forms?
There are philosophies of coming and going to
engage in, without actually moving your body.
There are economies and expenditures of being
to ponder: semiotics of to give it up, lend an ear.
So too with metaphors, symbolic representations
such as doors. While the main purpose of a door
is to admit, its secondary purpose is to exclude.
Will there be time to contemplate the grammar
of eternity in eternity? Are transhumanist and
Buddhist dreams of pure consciousness akin?
Last night, upon seeing my mother in hospice
for the first time in over a week, I crawled into
her bed and sobbed: a reality reality can't touch.
My father stood beside the bed, blessed likewise
by the gift of tears, the gift of death, the gift of
knowing that all knowing leads to unknowing.
I touched her skull, raised in parts by a shunt—
implanted to drain excess cerebrospinal fluid
from her brain—feeling her form like Braille.
There is grief, then there are theories of grief.
Also subjects, authored by an author of days.
I have spent my life on a thousand mindless,
inconsequential introductions, echo of hellos.
One day soon I will say goodbye to language
so she can ascend to an alternative universe
called heaven where there is no need of it:
where she is at peace, and perfectly loved.

2.

Provenance

I was born tiny, pink, and shrieking
from neonatal nicotine in the womb,
head encased by an auspicious caul.
Was supposed to be a boy, Luke.
Upon emerging, did they frown?
I grew up in a small Ohio suburb
that used to be a summer cottage
resort, and prior to that, was land
that belonged to the Erie Indians.
I had a doll, Debbie, I carried everywhere,
then in middle school, an invisible friend
I named Priscilla. I encouraged others
to believe in her: some did, in the way
certain children are willing to invest
in fantasy in order to remain alive.
A small house with little privacy,
I lived behind the couch, reading
with my cat, occasionally coming
out for meals that I poked at or fed,
sans observation, to the hungry dog.
I couldn't wrap my mind around
numbers, formulae, or geography,
preferring biographies of people
who blazed trails in their fields.
Adolescence hit like a meteor:
I became haunted and numb.
Decades later, I still feel I
have no recourse to forces
that railroad me without
my volition or consent.
I didn't ask to be born
I screamed at my mom,
when she called me out

for any minor infraction
turned major, with time.
Had I known now what
I couldn't know then, I
would have repeated it,
with theatrical aplomb.
The difference between
then and now is that now,
my life—mistake erased,
slipknot untied—is mine.

Symbiosis

There wasn't space for her to rebel
when we were younger, because she
couldn't bear to destroy my parents
with not one, but two, derelict girls.
I partied while she won tournaments,
studied, and planned for a future so
far from her past, that the only thing
recognizable about it was her smile.
Named after Anne of Green Gables,
a Canadian novel turned miniseries,
my father called her "steady Eddie,"
not knowing still waters run deeper
than erupting geysers of insurgency.
I taught her what I knew, not much:
how to flirt, drink, apply makeup,
muffle sobs in a shared bedroom.
To watch, as pain becomes armor,
then sedimentary rock: unbreakable
save for a miracle, wrested from time.
Confused with being identical twins,
our voices so similar we could fool
even our mother, our favorite prank.
The last child, alternately coddled
and forgotten, dreamy and stunned:
something about the orphan in her,
despite a near-religious devotion
to others, an ethics I didn't share.
When angry, harboring deep hurt,
she will do what the hero does:
refuse to answer letters, or care.
The first time her heart broke
she couldn't speak, causing
me to listen to Nina Simone

by her side. In the wailing,
I heard an anguish beyond
language, a shadowed cry.
She's the only reality I trust,
the visual world parading by.
She the raft, I the flooding:
our survival, synchronized.

Therapon

I'm a part of your story, you're a part of my story:
an endless bleed. My name a receipt for a purchase
on layaway uttered by people who don't love me,
rather the way I make them feel certain they need.
We're becoming machines, not only with labor but
cellularly: electromagnetic radiation and data feeds
polluting and rewriting our genetic histories until we
morph into automatons so hyperreal no one can even
tell the difference, not that there's anyone left outside.
I, a symptom of the age. I, walking human capital, still
capable of worship and grief, of phantasmagoric reverie.
I grew up in a suburban bubble fantasy hellscape where
everyone was a homecoming king or queen and spent a
fortune on real estate. My parents, who didn't care about
acquiring money nor manicured lawns, were reported by
neighbors and fined for not having a garage after the old
one crumbled, then again for having a loose dog, a mutt
my dad named Meatball that my sister foisted on them.
Can one not know one is being used? If this is a library,
where's the fire, what is the twisted logic behind cultural
acceleration and expansion or is it an infectious disease?
When the day takes the day away, where are we to rest,
hide, breathe? How can I bear a continuation of the same
plots and themes, without a change in tempo or intensity?
The devil doesn't want me to get to where I'm destined
to be: savage chaos precludes boundaries, rituals, truth.
I became one with my couch today and thought of you.
This is me trying not to be a dick. What I actually want
is for the dead to return, but my beloveds bade farewell.
I want an encounter, not a spectacle: want to be the hour
thought stops and power rises, a Shekhinah revelation of
a dream made tolerable by innovational pharmaceuticals,
lounging with my cat, and biting on leather amid screams.

Solar Plexus

Your upper chakras are phenomenal: the lower
ones are in trouble, an energy healer said to me.
But I already knew that, thanks to my open third
eye, the seat of intuition; chronic pain and anger;
and high vibrational frequency. Did you almost die
when you were born? she continued. Why yes, I did.
You were ambivalent about this incarnation, she said.
Still am, I said. This is my language: these my people.
And yet I only see them, if lucky, once in a blue moon,
which is to say, not enough to help me remember, nor
even want to remember, what it feels like to be human.
Isn't that what meaning is—the felt sense of the thing?
The solar plexus chakra's Sanskrit name is Manipura:
radiant jewel city ruled by the color yellow, and fire.
When balanced, you feel powerful: shining as a sun,
secure in your identity and focused on your purpose.
When weak, you feel insecure, directionless, fearful:
the light of consciousness flickering, unable to burn.
Is loving the good earth occultism? Is trying to honor
the body and its animating energy centers apostasy?
You don't need metaphor to see the animal you are.
You don't need to smell a rose to know its purpose
is purposelessness, coterminous with every beauty.
No one thinks they can withdraw from the theatre
of personal virtue, but guess what, folks: you can.
You can refuse to be the sacrificial bull, or lamb.
You can write your own name in magic marker
on the hegemons with your non-dominant hand.
And when the curtain lifts on the whole display,
you'll be off stage left, the event horizon razed:
mind clear as a lake on a cloudless summer day.

Ode to Inertia

Yesterday, I was defined by my resolute refusal
to entertain the vertical axis. Today, I look up,
gasp, and stare. I'm tired of arguing with God.
Tired of being told it's going to be a great one,
owing to an advantageous shift in climate crisis,
a door that locks, slapdash echolocation of birds.
A pathological relationship with the natural world
may entail a fear that nature will kill you, never
stepping outside, or bending to smell a flower,
performatively. It could involve complaining
all winter, only to complain more vociferously
on an inclement day in otherwise utopic spring.
Who am I to say, or judge? I'm just the narrator
of my life, expressing gratitude, but unfeelingly.
Day breaks, is divided into metronomic hours
of increasing busyness, as if inertia was a sin.
Look at Venus, slowest spinning body in the
known universe: she arrives at her destination,
nowhere, right on time. Like her, I want to lift
off from this whole damn stratosphere, relive
scenes from my youth in a poorly lit dive bar.
I want to exaggerate my movements and my
words, like a keynote speaker on ketamine.
I want to linger languorously, like perfume
on a woman you'll only see once but never
forget, until distracted by another woman.
I want to burn my to-do list, ceremonially,
scatter the ashes of the production machine.
The world won't fuck off until I'm no longer
in this world. How heaven-sent is death, or
heaven: what merciful quiet will that be.

Elegy

I left my heart at the gravesite
of my cat Elvira, killed on a road.
Before Elvira, I lost six other cats.
Their photos line my wall, in frames.
They are figures of sovereign innocence,
the impossible science of the unique being.
Is to know more about the world to know
more about terror, horror, and abjection?
To bear being seen, the recuperative gaze
of love that sees no flaw in the beloved
is a life labor: with Elvira, it happened
the second I cradled her, the moment
I said *you're home now, you're mine.*
Months passed, after she was taken,
when the only moving image I could
bear to see was raw uncut footage of
animals reunited with their owners,
or saved from peril—dogs, donkeys,
and snow leopards in mute ecstasy.
All of her cries were interrogative,
on earth: the world a question she
sought answers to. Driving home
last night, I pulled the visor down
to occlude the sun. And in its place
I saw her, the stable object of beauty
floating in the air, irrespective of my
position, comforting the comfortless.
Call it what you like, it's still there:
a silent, calm, ponderous presence
illuminating the heart's empty room.
I call it grief, call it Elvira, my baby,
call it mother, or what it is, the moon.

Fugue

It's been 212 days since you left this earth,
love, to enter the medieval ring of paradise.
Outside, the pothos shoots its alien blooms,
the trees leak sap from their arterial veins.
You're unrivaled, undefeated, as the one
who will never stop breaking my heart.
I wanted your death to never transpire,
or if it did, be an epiphany in the night.
The diminution of the objective world
condensed into an object on the floor,
cried *holy*, behold that square of light.
You were my prize, my high romance.
Draft after draft of my life hurried by:
cold excision, sheet music in the wind.
Until you arrived, a wayfaring vagrant
seeing shelter, like my umbilical twin.
We knew joy together, an infinity pool.
Your play toys, now artifacts of grief.
I want it to be conceptual, but it's not
conceptual. When you lose your mind,
you never really get it back. In truth, I
don't know who I am, why I am here,
but would suffer it all again for you.
To vouchsafe your existence, touch
your musky fur, feel your breathing
alter the planets—in your absence,
I call your name into the darkness.
Dead is dead, I discipline myself.
Consciousness sluicing through.

Midlife

Anything you can dream of having is
now a purchasable product. Do you
prefer eggs without whites? Here's
a carton of it, frothy yellow yolks.
Anything you can dream of doing
is harder to obtain, like becoming
president or running a marathon.
Me, I dream of who I want to be:
earthly catastrophe, personified;
a Roman goddess, unperturbed
by the immolation of your smile.
Not eating when you're not hungry
is a sign of nobility, but the bar is low
after the advent of digital colonialism.
My best and worst lover was cocaine,
because it made me a better worker.
I loved it to distraction, to excess,
to the point of overdosing while
driving, saved by a friend who
followed me home. After he
carried my unconscious body
to my apartment, I mumbled
thanks then slept it off, only
to do more the following day.
Hard not to see the years that
followed as dull by contrast,
my brain always dialing back
to near-death experiences as a
litmus test of what it means to
feel alive. Now I look up at the
moon in her serial completion
knowing states of unbecoming
only appear as such to humans:

untrained in what is everlasting,
the fine arts of how not to die.

Ex-Voto

After the light Blake calls experience,
after the day's attrition, after acrid heat,
after yet another lonely, unbillable hour
comes the rough scrim of evening tide.
I have no more opinions about it than
a tree would have about its expansion
by a ring: no more regrets than I have
about the passing of the vainglorious
past, a nonevent I didn't see coming.
O cocaine, won't you tell me, when
I wake and only my dream remains
who I am, sheared of my golden mane?
I want what dulls pain receptors in the
brain, or blocks nerves from sending
the signals of pain: a modest request,
like beauty, a pleasing centerpiece
distracting guests from their food.
Is to be iterative to become a brand?
Is there a nuclear manness, to man?
Were it not for the body, there would
be no documentation of time in nature.
I reach for the ibuprofen to palliate the
violence, cruelty, and crises of the age.
I miss you like I miss speech, which is
to say like breathing, my favorite drug,
and not at all. Pleasure is my phantom
limb, my casino win, sinner's prayer:
what I surrendered to fulfil my vows.
Now I'm stitched to this world as if
it was the only world, dispassionately,
waiting for a dopamine surge to ignite.
Even nuns need feel-good chemicals.
Don't get me wrong, God: I love not
the metaphorical dark, but the night.

Convert

So much of life is utter bullshit.
I say this as someone who used
to foot the bill, lead the charge.
In my recurring dream of unpaid
prostitution, I only realize I was
exploited when I've already fled
the scene. Give me my labor back,
the blank space where life should be.
I'm half-drunk on gin, writing in tears.
Translate me, and don't translate me.
A faithful translation is one in which
the translator's hand never appears.
Do you remember when I used to be
confident and adventurous? Vaguely,
watercolor stain on a concave mirror.
The wolves of obsolescence are hungry.
See you soon: a euphemism for get lost.
Nature tries to recall our higher selves,
but we're too busy valorizing business.
The mountain stands tall, mountaining.
The deer adopts a species not her own.
My dislikes are many, affinities few:
I like songs to which I can sing along,
my family, and solfeggio frequencies.
Alone, loneliness is never a thought
until intercepted by a rattling door,
the odor of a man. No woman needs
intercourse: few women escape it.
Thankfully, I'm a vegetarian now.
Then there's language over there,
failed enterprise. You can't eat it,
you can't fuck it, it's not beautiful.
And yet, like a cosmos, it survives.

Applicant

I've caught glimpses of infinite potential,
yes—transcendental awareness, and pure,
reverential love. You can't save everyone,
however, or make everyone stupid happy.
The sea's sensuous depths, the materiality
of money, and time's bent arrow interfere.
I am not well enough to perform my duties,
I said to my boss. He said, do them anyway.
As a teen, I worked at Bed Bath & Beyond.
I wandered around housewares, hoping to be
helpful to someone looking to buy a crockpot.
Later came jobs as a nanny, typist, and barista,
surrounded by the din of children and machines.
At night, I close my eyes, and I'm propelled into
space, where I don't have to oblige or indulge the
man, as in an episode of *Cheers*, where everyone
knows my name despite my efforts at anonymity.
I unclasp my bra alone, curse alone, clean alone.
At every interview I now undergo, I'm rejected,
rudely disqualified by the shred of a point again.
Do you think I was made for, or long to belong
to this world, a parade of melodramatic scenes?
Like the time my ex-husband and I wrote our
initials in the sand on our Kauai honeymoon,
then photographed it, thinking about forever:
the tide erased it, and later, my memory too.
Show me the way, Google, to my best life.
Watch over my ongoing commodification:
hold me in your gaze, the way lovers do.

Intercession

The past is always arriving.
The future is so seldom here.
And the present, a perfect storm,
thrashes madly but won't appear.
What I want recedes on a wave
that is not a wave, only water.
What I want is the inverse of
what everyone else seems to want:
to get what they think they deserve.
Take poetry: you have to be rich,
in some sense, to write a poem,
which is to say you have time
to luxuriate in hypotheticals.
I don't have time: I steal it
from the overlord of labor,
pleasure's puppet master.
I make a loud commotion
then disappear when he
is assessing the damage
to his surf & turf dinner,
his gold-encrusted valise.
How much grief is too
much: is there a surfeit,
a cap that engenders no?
Make me like the moon.
She never begs, even before
being beheaded without trial.
Make me like the sun, who
cannot be thwarted in any
true cosmological sense.
No one wants the real you?
No one wants the real me, either.
No one wants the real anyone:
Lord, have mercy on us all.

Lamentation

Please take a moment to fill out these forms.
Six hours later, yes, the forms have been filled.
I've drank the bitter cup, eaten bread of sorrow,
lived to know that work is bad for your health.
The paperwork enshrouding it, the routine bills
and insurance premiums justifying it, like a kick
in the teeth of a thoroughly benumbed stud horse,
whose only value is to generate seed, as decreed.
Expecting someone from the slacker generation
to work 60-hour weeks and be delighted about it
is an unwholesome delusion in need of crushing.
Wealth as having an extra bag of boiled rice is a
measure of economic progress I long to surpass.
Am I more than the sum of every high and low?
Will He who smote great nations, slew mighty
kings, majestically vanquish my enemies, too?
Other than a couple awkward hugs, I have not
been touched in years. Forgive me, my body
has not been touched in years, thanks to the
invisible fencing I professionally installed,
otherwise known as an energetic boundary.
Words make or break us: bring peace, war.
I hold my phone like it's a chalice or vessel,
when really it's just a phone. What portent,
what auspicious omen do I expect to come,
funnelling through electromagnetic smog?
Gadgets jockey for my precious attention,
already subdivided like a federal territory.
Giants fall, mountains move, waters part:
no further proof is needed of God, I see.
I click to insert my signature, whereof I'm
glad: thou hast dealt bountifully with me.

Fin du Monde

A sea of faces incites nausea: they look like
baby birds waiting for their mother's worm.
Flies buzz around me, thinking I'm carnage,
or enjoying my Bois de Balincourt perfume.
I sit and observe friends networked to death,
as if people watching at the Tate or Louvre.
Theirs, a brief effusion, brief as these words:
experience, memory, perception, exchanged
for chronic interconnectedness, surveillance,
former democratic rule turned demagoguery.
The ice outside forms into glittery stalactites,
like stilettos hung from trees. Perforce I must
be plain: there exist angels at the intersection,
angels at the stoplight, angels in cyclonic rain.
Angels fortify ramparts, defending the queen,
on the ceremonial parade grounds of mystery.
I saw one at a flower stall in Poland: another
at Souk des Teinturiers, a Marrakesh bazaar.
They throng the Lord, interceding as ghosts
or thieves. Why did I cry today for an hour,
with my whole body, the way babies cry?
Because I saw how beings more innocent
than babies are tortured, all the world over:
animals that once swam, ran, and breathed.
It feels criminal to turn from this suffering:
a fate beyond language, worse than death.
Outside my window, a destroyed birch's
trunk mimics a ballerina in first position,
when in truth that's a weather-beaten tree.
As for those who seek recognition: they have
their reward. It is finished, the forestalled end.
At last I'll see my hunger for meaning go free.

Metaphysical

The earth is rotating, time flying, and space bending
while I'm taken apart and reassembled in many gazes,
including my own. Historically, the word *want* implies
a lack or deficiency. Do I want for something? Why yes.
Four corners of a mud hut, steady income, a few secure
attachments, water and bread. I have no use for beauty,
which, like real wealth, or want, is hidden from view.
Yesterday, I followed a long, forested driveway, past
private property signs, just to see where it would lead.
A millionaire's compound arose in the mist, a mirage
inhabited by those who have no need of transparency,
nestled away in that deep inaction where music reigns.
Parmenides denied change altogether, believing that in
the way of truth, reality is one, and existence timeless
and uniform. Zeno, also a monist philosopher, agreed,
arguing that travel spanning any finite distance can be
neither completed nor begun, so all motion is illusory
when considering time as composed solely of instants.
Centuries later, Henri Bergson introduced a theory of
time and consciousness, *la durée*, in response to Kant
and the pre-Socratic philosophers, after realizing that
the moment someone attempts to measure a moment,
it disappears, as for the individual, time speeds up or
slows down, whereas for science, it remains the same.
Despite the demonstrated observer effect in quantum
theory, emphasizing the participation of subjectivity,
Bergson and Einstein disagreed on the nature of time:
Einstein considering Bergson's views to be that of a
soft psychology, irreconcilable with the quantitative

realities of physics, while Bergson thought Einstein's
theory of time was metaphysics grafted onto science,
one that denied the ineffable, intuitive aspect of time.
I stare into the middle distance at the Greek goddess
of truth, Aletheia, a word that translates as revealing,
disclosure, unconcealment: distinct from veiled Isis,
Moses' veil, and the tabernacle veil, protecting God's
people from his fierce, wrathful fire, until the temple
veil was torn at Jesus' death, signifying his death
and the promise of restoration to God's presence.
The horses of Achilles were Xanthus and Balius:
epic offspring of Zephyrus, god of the west wind,
they were immortal and could speak. I, too, was
fixed to that chariot in war. When Patroclus, who
fed and groomed them, died, they stood beside the
Trojan battlefield together, motionless, and wept.
What is it about grief that turns a heart to stone?
I sit alone, consider stillness: in this immobility
I look, see, and do not desire, for I am content
to think about the end, and of want, being here.
Before apokatastasis, a dramatic complication,
but I'm weary of plot contrivances and scenes.
I want to stop time so that I can live within it—
awaken to a new world, a snow globe shaken.
To run the race, then return to the primordial
garden of existence: naked figures in a dream.

Childlessness

I lie horizontal and think about the rain,
how the garden has not yet been seeded.
Above, a storm cloud floats, an ambient
drone, joining others in a convocation
of whatever my mind imagines them
to be: a velociraptor, brain aneurism,
Jehovah on his throne. I have no need
to see myself replicated or reproduced,
however, let alone genetically spliced
with a man who will break my heart:
have no desire for a form of laboring
that would split me open like an atom,
nor to raise a small human who learns
how to exist by neuronally mirroring
my ways of existing, from behavior
to the inflections and pitch of voice.
Creation and self-forgetting cannot
coexist when you bring a child or
children into the world, because
now your name is father, mother:
species survival depends on this
willingness to remain one thing.
Yet to be any form, what is that?
Proteus, the god of shapeshifting,
can foretell the future but changes
his shape to avoid said prophecies:
answering solely to those capable
of capturing and holding him while
he morphs between a lion, serpent,
leopard, water, tree. I don't know.
I think change is hard, personally.
I'm not selfish: I'm impoverished.
Therefore, my lifework will be me.

Verisimilitude

The cold, the dark, the future—the terror
of the vast unknown shudders my bones.
Dawn breaks. I stand at the promontory
of a home I do not own, at a landscape
grown foreign with winter's embrace:
the rustling leaves, propelled by wind,
trick my eye, espied first as sparrows,
the trees grow more spindly by night.
I am more than halfway through life,
a fact only recently arrived as a fact.
I palm it, the inevitability of a death,
sorrows and regrets that accompany
youth's passing, a touristic souvenir.
Beauty was posited as a capital good;
adjectival clauses, deployed liberally;
banquets could not fail to disappoint
a mind fattened on anticipatory hope.
Lower your expectations, a therapist
once advised: for you and others too.
As if ambition's end were peaceable.
As if the crows in the yard, knowing
nothing of the making of money, the
handling of money, the exchange of
money for goods and services, care
about the manufacture of happiness,
the illusion of destination: they don't.
One finds the remainder of my meal,
cries out to alert its family of harvest,
which is to say of something provided
rather than scavenged: taste of manna
from an otherworldly source that flees.
They bear what I cannot, without pride.
The flock is gone as quickly as it came.

What I've done for a paycheck, my god.
What I've spent it on is scattered abroad
in the bodies of living shadows, memory.

Black Hole

I'm sick of my face. Can I take it off,
mask of pantyhose worn by a thief?
Can I trade up, for museum beauty
or airbrushed celebrity perfection?
Those faces don't crinkle or age:
they shine bright as headlights of
an SUV careening down the Autobahn
en route to mecca or the Lower Rhine.
My face resounds, reduplicates, divides.
If an equation, it's the string of symbols
devised by Einstein to describe a theory
of general relativity: the left-hand side
pictorializes the geometry of space-time,
the right-hand side, all mass and energy.
Information is not knowledge, he wrote:
knowledge's only source is experience.
My face is tired of experience, sapped
by being gaslit out of my true feelings:
rage, reverence, adoration, antipathy.
My ancestors, mostly potato farmers
from hardy Eastern European stock,
speak out of my face like prophets
in search of an incarnate messiah,
my face a burning bush or wheel.
You view my administrative face:
its abandonment during the throes
of passion is also a mystery to me.
Sad, slumping face, consternated
face overwrought by cognition,
face upturned with dumb hope:
I trace your origins, relentlessly.
When my ex-husband called me
a black hole, he was, in a sense,

correct: my face a gravity field
so strong even light cannot beam.
Supernova explosion, neutron star,
lead me to a beyond, deep within:
eros of the unthought, undreamed.

Pegasus

Peace as a silencing of automated control.
Pleasure as the body's proximity to itself.
Joy as watching the light dragged through
the dusty blinds, making shapes on a wall.
The case is closed, many grievances aired.
That there's so many of you is my concern.
For every answered call, another ten arrive,
all with different demands and exigencies.
If money isn't an index of value, what is?
At my autopsy, traces of substances the
governing body calls illicit were found.
I bought a product that simulates tears
to express my condolences I couldn't
perform to your expectations without
help from the beer guy, the drug guy.
Never came close to matching with
the job description's qualifications,
anyway, though God knows I tried.
Tried to be efficient, or reasonable,
but merit flew from my hands like
sand through a hourglass or sieve.
I don't mind losing things as long
as I know where they are, including
my mind long ago petrified in stone.
I don't believe in emotions anymore,
or any amplification of high fantasy.
The muses were born when Pegasus
stamped his hooves on the ground,
from flowing springs on Helicon.
That's when I knew I could breathe—
when my body left its elliptical orbit
and was, from the world's grip, free.

Relic

I had a lover who told me my looks
were classic, then changed his mind,
amending the description to "relic":
an object surviving from an earlier
time, especially one of historical or
sentimental interest. I had never felt
so seen. Who is the fleet's admiral?
What's heavier than a gold crown?
If forced to choose between auto
and manual, I will choose manual:
I don't place my trust in machines.
God Bless America: shit fiction,
high stakes of low-hanging fruit,
doomsday on loop, ill-conceived.
How could I seek the world again?
The ocean is a more faithful mirror
than an actual mirror could ever be.
To help dying people, you must be
solid and fearless. The body, mind,
and senses preside, impermanently.
My love isn't your love, it's mine:
off-grid like an extraterrestrial,
debating the careers of flowers,
waiting for the drugs to kick in.
Relic: from the Latin *reliquiae*,
meaning remains, as in stays,
but also personal effects left
behind after lights dim down.
We must become godlike, not
in power but in vulnerability.
No one can stare at the sun,
and no one remains too long.
Water my seeds of happiness:
be thou my strength and song.

3.

Antiphon

I cannot remember a time when I was not chosen last.
That and the great, timeless subjects: music, weather, war.
Wounds are openings through which presence shines through.
The child in the doll, Christ in the wafer, the ocean in a droplet.
The photos of beloveds I store in a keepsake box, under the bed.
A heaven without animals, the body and its angel: burial grounds.
My body was dialogue and forgiveness. My body was a hovercraft,
motherless, confusing the distinction between epitaph and epigraph.
I pity the meat that carnivores eat: how it died for them, will not rise.
Call it the underworld, call it sleep. The heart clenched, whooshing
blood to the rest of the system, untouched by Anthropocenic grief.
The world bloomed, phosphorescent: black and blue, like a bruise.
I will go back to events commemorating life one day, fictitiously.
Weightless as a cumulous cloud, heavy as the infinitive to weep.
The widow is singular at night, putting out milk for her children
through the lattice of trees in the dark theatre of a broken chord.
Fast food joints occupy street corners where church used to be.
No self-statements are true, and the righteous won't be moved.
I do not believe in happiness, unless by happy, you mean free.

Apocalypse

Tell me: do you, too, feel
dead yet have to expend
twice the inertial energy
pretending you're alive?
Do you, too, know that
existence is over, though
we have to continue our
shared belief in things like
academic institutions and
payroll, biotech, and wars,
in order to try to survive?
How do you express that
to your mother? How,
to your lover, in the
shock of new sight,
or long recognized?
We have never not
been modern, nor
will we ever be:
getting a foothold
into actual living
remains the quest
of all philosophy.
Knowing enough
is comprehension:
learning how to
surrender gently,
the heart of song.
Baby, bills are due.
Baby, we're having
a baby. And thus,
the world goes on.

Pilgrim

What does it mean to be ambitious:
beautiful people exercising options?
Waiting for the light to change, then
gunning it past another designer car?
I have read the terms and conditions.
I have waited at the pharmacy for my
birth control and dopamine blockers,
then wondered why I feel like hell.
If quest is at the heart of romance,
is brokenness at the heart of quest?
Your call will be answered in the order
it was received. Stillness of pavement,
immensity of planets and the vast gasp
between them, asteroids raining down.
The nuclear self is a convenient truth.
Once I saw a man beating his mailbox
with a closed fist. It feels right to tell
you this: we answer to God at the end
of our lives, like a magnet to its filling.
He beautifies the weak with salvation,
turns our minds from perishable things.
Laugh a little, friend. Oh, I'm laughing,
with no point of reference, nervously.
Warning: viewer discretion advised.
The world, the flesh, and the devil
inveigh me cruelly from the stands.
Remove me from those liars, Lord:
forsake not the work of thy hands.

Cogito

I will never fully understand the discourses
around thinking. What should I be thinking
about: what eggheads are thinking about?
What other people are thinking about me?
Furthermore, why tell someone what you
are thinking about? Isn't that the last secret,
in this denuded, dematerialized world, that
should be dearly prized, winsomely sung—
one that you wouldn't give away for free?
A beautiful thought is a very beautiful thing.
If one more day in my life happens without
intentionality, another is pulling the strings.
I've done nothing today to improve my lot
or luck, nor earn a single dollar, but as well,
nor have I spent, on what the world thinks
of as necessary or luxury goods. I think
Jesus sets the bar impossibly high, but
that's why I love him: lonesome bird,
pointing at the sky. The problems you
have and the problems you think you
have are not the same. You can't
bum-rush an elevator. You can't
expect anyone to understand a life
other than their own. The queries
are so many, the answers so few.
If relationships have a rhythm,
our rhythm was tectonic, alive.
The world is gone, I carry you.
It might've all been in my head,
but Lord, what a ride.

Human Resources

I am the place where thinking was.
I don't face the world, I face a wall.
If I were a librarian, at least I would
know a thing or two about indexing.
As it stands, I'm a one-size-fits-all
garment made cheaply in a country
where the workers can't afford food.
What is the cash nexus between us?
If I dance the Macarena at a wedding,
leading the tribe into stupefied oblivion,
will eligible suitors also propose to me?
I saved the village of myself by cutting
down trees and known power supplies.
I hid my saber tooth, my buffalo skull,
my last precious cache of good ovaries:
refusing to go to market and stand there
while some dipshit eyeballs my wares,
severing the bond between intimacies.
I want to dig a hole so deep that I forget
the point of digging is to lay foundation
for an edifice or unearth what's buried.
Digging just to dig, like a maniac dog,
beyond all administrative bureaucracy.
I open my mouth and junk pours out.
I run the numbers, fuss with the font.
When asked for my hours by payroll,
I hand them a shattered crystal ball,
tell them money is an illusion, like
the future, and happiness, and God.

Sturm und Drang

This is my horse, abstraction.
He is white, with gelid wings.
The thingness of a thing,
the thisness of the world, yes—
but is there a cause, a design?
Positive thoughts are delusions,
as are negative, suicidal thoughts.
Cosmic events such as supermoons
only appear as such to the human eye.
The only reward for working faster
is more work: embodied labor
extracted from faulty machines,
downloading data irrespective
of time, space, a body or soul.
Some prayers are unanswered,
others beyond the scope of hope:
living on a habitable planet is one.
That's the way of matter, I guess.
I took three multivitamins today.
Is that pollution or vapor from a hot dog stand?
Is he a happy drunk or a person without a home?
Undercut the competition, produce at all costs:
I know the script by heart, its imperative mood.
Give me your worst, I said to god:
disease, torment, cruelty, accident.
Death, if it should please you, too.
Me, I like the sensation of falling:
neutral light, as if from a screen
floods the sky, passing through.

Carpe Diem

Look, mother, I made a cultural object. Look, father,
the dialectic is breaking down again, replaced by the
narcotic of toxic positivity and promulgated screeds.
I open a relevant magazine: themes explored include
obesity, the spirit world, colonialism, and drone wars.
I open my closet: on the top shelf, a crown of thorns.
Technology is undertheorized. It's been a ramen year.
If forced to choose between a good trip and a bad trip,
I roll the dice toward reality, brace for unending pain.
After a senseless death, I felt the need to speak again.
This is an attempt to collect a debt. Anything you say
can be used against you, or else monitored for quality
assurance purposes. Pummeled by assholes, I faint
then rise, on the slow tides of history and calamity:
an adult makes 35,000 conscious decisions per day.
But I am but a child, face bright with the old truth.
I offer you my offline self, god, a dignifying word.
How lifelike, a candle lit by light-emitting diodes.
How beautiful, the floral arrangement of eternity.
I feel I'm near the end, but that's just a feeling.
What other transformation would it be.

Doxology

And then—sunburst through clouds.
And then acute feels, of propinquity.
I like the text; it's the subtext I have
issues with, the hollowing out of my
innards when the last friend leaves.
I have no interest in paying off the
interest, nor the principal, on debt.
I am unamused by abstract notions,
plot-based novels, and constituencies.
Being single is a gift that keeps giving,
however: howling in the moribund fog,
wearing athleisure gear to formal events,
pacing the floor at 3 a.m. like Hamlet, mad,
perfecting the naked body for you alone.
In a world with no hell to follow, I will
no longer be attracted, phenomenally
or pheromonally, to any person, nor
will I have the occasion to even meet
them, reluctant as I am to quit my flat
and stake out claims in the wild world
of endless subterfuge and wandering,
lost souls claiming to be found until
they meet their maker in this life,
or another, however alarmingly.
Every hour is an hour of truth:
selfhood a category erased,
while auctioneers quibble
for the remains of mind.
Sad mammal, analogue
girl in a virtual world:
people are just guessing.
Let us be tender and kind.

Overture

If the heart is a temple,
each statue will be broken.
But I have practiced idolatry:
loved the creature more than
the creator, whom I can't see.
There's a hole where the sun
should be. It has entered me,
along with the cloud and river.
I am like an actor, requesting
for their character to be killed.
Can life be had, unmediated?
Turning away and touching
are both wrong, raging fires.
Forms of quest and deferral,
rooms of angels and ghosts.
It takes me a day to recall
the old melodies, pitched
timbrels of lute and lyre.
It's only vulgar to speak
about money if you have
none: same with desire.
Addictive technologies,
the myths and metaphors
we fail to adequately serve.
I touch my uterus, not really.
A patina of dust settles quietly
over the assembled memories.
To put it delicately, there is no
greater way. To put it delicately,
the price of love is always grief.
Have a great weekend. I'm fine.
I open my hymnal: *by the time*
the waves reach you, they will
no longer be waves, reformed
into proportions of My design.

Prelude

Most of my life has been a spectacular failure.
I only wanted to eliminate the margin of error
in the bowels of the earth, or in unseen realms.
May the force be with you. And you, and you.
Beneath are the everlasting arms. I will rest
in them, until instituting a controlled burn.
For we know in part, and prophesy in part.
But one day, lining up the porcelain china,
thinking of the adventures that lovers are
having without you, you will be affirmed.
Mistakes: a lesson in epistemic humility.
The faucet's steady drip, the banker's
ironclad grip: songs of unbecoming.
Think of Mozart, wild with sorrow,
dodging debtors, and out of work.
The hardest thing I've ever done
in my life, is live. In due season,
I entered the realm of misfortune,
where tragedy became possible
rather than a passing anecdote.
I know why I'm happy now:
I have no more cows to lose.
Prefect with predatorial fangs:
I'm not paralyzed, I'm praying,
surrounded by avarice and hate,
dead kings encrusted with gold.
I'll try my hand at calligraphy;
unfeel my feelings; buy fabrics,
like linen, that breathe and give.
What could be more beautiful
than being introduced by music?
I need another life to get it right,
to inaugurate the impossible again.

Sonata

This is a torn map of the forsaken world.
There are lines even wolves cannot cross.
Every voice an epitaph, then a little tune
from the neighbor's garden apartment
suggesting a rondo, or circle of fifths.
Plato said the soul is a perfect circle.
Perfection: from the Latin *perfectus,*
meaning a hollow object, complete.
When a child, I spoke as a child.
Then I clung to childish things.
String theory, interconnection,
held fast by grace and gravity:
that, too, has occurred to me.
The trick is to stay embodied:
seeking guidance, blessings,
or propitiation from the gods.
I spread the atlas on the floor,
confuse it again with territory.
There's no allegorical signifier
for which God stands, except
the market's invisible hand.
I don't feel crazy today, but
the light streaming through
the windows accentuates
the dirt-caked surfaces,
the intervening themes.
When Schubert passed
of typhoid fever at 31,
he left us a vast oeuvre,
an unfinished symphony.

Coda

If nirvana is the extinction of concepts,
and graduate school the acquisition
of concepts, the only justification
for denying myself enlightenment
is getting a job, which I don't have.
Does this make me a jedi ninja or
a consummate loser? How sweet,
the pathogenic air on my sleeves.
The art of today is marketized,
beyond Apollo and Dionysus,
without a baseline of quality.
Who lives here? Is this my life?
How can one love without ideas?
Maybe I took the wrong pills again.
Maybe I confused changing channels
with dismantling the primitive machine.
If thoughts are energy, and anger illusion,
what forms of verisimilitude are left to me?
I can't believe the shit that God puts up with.
Take my never-ending freight train of bullshit.
Take my prayer to be accountable, followed by
a burning desire to sing mermaid songs all day.
For dinner, I ate two fish fingers: once frozen,
made edible by the true miracle of convection.
After the funeral, I hurried to put on my jeans.
The cedars of Lebanon are aromatic and durable.
The neon sign blinks *we buy gold.* Who is we?
Yet I am responsive to him; his way is perfect.
As for your days, so shall your strength will be.

Optimism

Is that a house, or an AI-generated image?
Is that a face, or a high-resolution dream?
Father, agent of my solitude, deliver me
from this silent passion play, wherein I'm
typecast as a grieving witness in the crowd.
Pain made me conscious of my need of you,
as if I had to know dependency to praise you.
I was empty, then: filled with the words and
ideas of others, vulnerable to hungry wolves.
I was the world's plaything, eager to please,
to echo and anticipate the desires of others,
that in exceeding them I might be fulfilled.
Instead of rewriting my story, you erased
my story—husband, lover, stranger, god—
subtle distinctions feel meaningless now,
my body a sunken depression in the grass.
Sweaty palms, palpitating heart, cognitive distortions:
what on earth has ever been accomplished by desire?
The songs feel alien: the unspeakable entered them.
There is a hole in the ozone. I do not own my name.
A god falls in love with a mortal: both live forever.
A mortal falls in love with a mortal: after the spell
follows misery, decrepitude, the end of the flame.
I didn't write this bummer opera: it wrote itself,
fatalism styled as choose your own adventure.
I'm dead now, nothing hurts. I ask you what
every soul in purgatory asks: will I be raised?

Antithesis

I'm not paying retail. I'm not
your doormat, footstool, scourge.
Clean up after your own catastrophe:
I'm not offshored labor, or a sponge.
I'm not waiting in line for ten hours
to see a doctor about my condition.
I'll carry my broken bones with me
instead, test results of abnormality.
I hope you're ok, but as is evident,
I'm not you. I don't belong in this
madhouse, I said to the psych ward
attendant: I'm not mad, just touched
by the next world's prescient hymns.
He disagreed, after I threw a broom
and papered the wall with post-its
translating *help* in twelve tongues.
I am not art at the Venice Biennale,
nor the makers, sponsors, or crowd,
not bait nor animals trapped therein.
Once when I bought a photo frame
I left the stock photo in, to remind
myself I have family everywhere:
in Detroit and the deserts of Sinai.
But with work, I'm not delusional:
I take account of me, as an entity,
the way Judith Butler proscribed.
I am not Judith Butler, however,
not a subject opaque to myself
nor gender performed or made.
I'd like to be a hood ornament,
Rolls-Royce's Spirit of Ecstasy.
Three inches tall, in gold-plated
flowing robes, she represents a

spiritual direction for the brand,
serenity of a product in motion,
but I am not a goddess of speed:
I move, if at all, as mountains do.
Village idiot, mutant, holy fool—
I am at your mercy and service,
god: I am nothing, without you.

Anemone

The white anemone is a cruel gift, Father.
A perennial, it's born to die, and not return.
Anemone, Greek for "daughter of the wind."
Something must have happened to the mother,
stewards of the earth say, when seeing a litter
of kittens, bunnies, squirrels, or baby birds
fallen from the sky. We mimic her motions,
her fastidious hovering, maternal diligence,
hoping abandoned fledglings might survive.
My sister wound a plastic flower at the foot
of my mother's hospice bed, to bring cheer.
I adjusted the curtains: is it too much light?
Not enough? She stared at and through me,
unable to have or articulate her preference.
Instead, I spoke, because she could hear.
In heaven, nothing changes, save for the
concealing and magnifying of presence.
I can picture it, a bucolic pastoral scene:
shepherdess herding cows by your side.
Yet with a single turn of fortune's wheel
I found myself impersonal and asexual:
no known next-of-kin, no cause or cure.
I don't steal, I don't harm or hit anyone.
I routinely act irrespective of how I feel.
For what am I preparing: my own death?
Forgive me, please, for misrecognition,
for preferring to stand alone in a field.
I thought to save you by saving myself,
which I know is the saddest departing.
The more I become myself, the more I
betray the world.

Requiem

This is my mass for the dead, sung into
a multitude of single-person dwellings
which at night, from an aerial perspective,
light up the landscape like an electrical fire.
Most pain is merely psychological, regardless,
and who needs excess when you have enough?
What was left to me: a portrait of the Madonna
and child in a crown, surrounded by impassive
art lovers, reflecting on the tempura or gold.
Look outside: what you see is propaganda.
It feels personal, which like any illusion,
cannot be. Elohim, Adonai, El Shaddai—
the only thing that hurts worse than loss
is losing you, progenitor of my dreams.
The dead wave, expecting a response.
But I too am waiting for an indication,
the night to which your voice belongs.
I have made peace with impermanence,
the dark-eyed juncos twittering in space:
who I'll become when I'm no longer me.
If you inhabit the praises of your people,
I will praise you, not the mutilated world.
Who else can breathe into dust and create a body,
speak into nothing and make something appear?
Your word a new holy land, some long promise
I dredge forth letter by letter, until by that song,
a future untold by graves innumerable, I can see.

Amor Fati

I touched a moth's wing while cleaning,
thinking to remove its deceased form.
It fluttered and awoke: I pulled back,
shocked it was not dead, but sleeping.
I've found sleeping moths, since then,
everywhere: Atlas, Hercules, Ornate,
Luna, White Witch, Wax, on counters,
crevices, and walls. They flock through
an open window and find shelter here.
When unable to find a light source at
night, whether lunar or a porch lamp,
they navigate by geomagnetic signals
created by the earth's electric current.
Positively phototactic, they love light
because they're evolved to maintain
a constant angle to the source of the
sun or moon, thus spiraling toward
artificial light as if a celestial body,
their navigational system confused.
Rest awhile, weary travelers, along
with the beetles, mosquitos, spiders,
ants, and flies: I'll not do you harm.
Moths, like butterflies, birds, bees,
are pollinators for flowering plants,
providing a key ecosystem service
in supporting terrestrial production:
endangerments to their population
poses a threat to global food webs,
biodiversity, and human survival.
Tiger, Carpet, Peppered, and Silk
of industrial fame: may your fate
not be an illusion, drawn upward
toward the all-consuming flame.

Gloria Patri

Glory be to god for septic tanks, drainage pipes:
for conversions thermodynamic and of the soul.
Glory be to god for this quiet, cheap hotel room:
only music the mini-fridge's vibratory drone,
creaky plumbing groaning through the walls.
We underestimate the perfect peace of objects.
Before me was another traveler: after I leave,
hundreds of others will arrive, anonymously,
drink sink water from disposable plastic cups,
recline on bleached sheets, stare into the void
of a generic landscape painting across the bed
while contemplating the disaster of their lives.
And when the alarm wails hours before dawn,
human cusses of angry protest join the chorus
of budget appliances failing before their time.
Why even look at a clock? It's never good news.
It takes the time it takes, my estimated deadline,
which is likely why no employer would trust me
to lead their staff toward an optimized wet dream.
I'm at an age where everyone around me is dying.
I'm at an age when the recited script isn't enough.
Glory be to god for logjams, the antediluvian dark,
for being a supply of goodness outpacing demand
because so many prefer their egos' endless ranting
to the suggestion of a different narrator or narrative.
Me, I am so clearly incapable of leading a brigade.
I'm glad to accept help in whatever form it comes:
hour of privacy within these semen-sprayed walls,
deadbolt securing my safety from the chaos outside
and the strivings of the people which are everywhere.
I can't point to you on a map: don't know your name
or from whence you came. But flames lick the canvas
and I acknowledge my poverty of being and my need.

Glory be to god for this unforgiving mirror, this soap,
this Gideon Bible tucked away in the bedside drawer:
whoever dwells in the secret place of the most High
will abide under the shadow of the Almighty, I read.
A freely given gift whose only precondition is belief,
it was put there for safekeeping, for salesmen like me.

Vespers

To seek to uncomplicate,
to make the unseen seen,
to receive but not consume:
if there is a higher order here,
news of which has not arrived.
Like a bright exhalation in the evening,
I hear the starlings singing each to each.
At the limit of my perception, awareness:
at recognition's edge, consciousness of
pleasure as more than absence of pain.
The body resists, prefers the basement
to deliverance, stiffens against the wind.
Go, urges the mind, above an even row
of dwarf boxwood. *Too many variables,*
the body responds, while the soul waits,
as it's waited for eternity, in a show ring:
staring at its image in a three-way mirror.
Surely by predestination you signify fate,
whose orchestration can't be manipulated.
No one plans a trip to the emergency room.
No one succeeds, wiping shadows off a wall.
I feel small, like a blotch of ink on rice paper.
I watch objects flail, awaiting the mastery of
a hand. I don't want to do it like I did before.
I want to be a dynamic character, capable of
change, driven toward progress, a linear goal.
Bring thinking under the obedience of Christ,
whose thoughts are greater than those below.
And then, a quiet movement through stasis—
clean lines of the horizon merge, a portrait
of someone I don't know coming into view.
What else is love but a vertiginous violence?
Intimacy with myself prepared me for you.

Breviary

At the time of her death, I was driving to see her.
When told, I pierced the air with primal screams.
Upon racing into the room, her skin barely sallow,
I laid across her body weeping, passage confirmed.
That's not her, my brother said. And yet once it was.
He opened the window to let her spirit fly away free.
At the wake, her casket was coronated with flowers.
I read her Corinthians, Dickinson, Langston Hughes.
Her friend said, How can the dearest person be gone?
Another rejoined, Your mom always worried for you.
At the funeral mass, my father asked me to tie his tie.
A parishioner approached, and asked him who died.
My wife, he said, every word an elevation to climb.
Our beloved sister in Jesus, faithful servant of God,
murmured the priest, will, like Lazarus, rise again.
Six pallbearers carried her, anointed, to the hearse,
through grey skies, fog, an inscrutable veil of rain.
I'm so sorry for your loss, a knife prolonging pain,
blank leitmotif of grief, wrong arms embracing me:
the consoler and the inconsolable rudderless at sea,
watching unforeseen tragedies congeal into history.
Now I see funeral homes everywhere, lighthouses
recalling that all mortal flames will go to their rest.
Now I begin the day by saying her name, Theresa,
asking her what were her dreams, how she slept.
At noon I light a candle, editorialize my actions
so she knows she is within, more than memory.
I vow to preserve your peace, no further unease.
If you knew her, you'd know she could never die,
would never leave us here alone in a pit of despair.
Like a child asking existential questions, I call out
Can you hear me? Are you joyful? Are you there?
Do not believe these lies they are telling, mother.

They don't know you are alive in every goodness,
every wink, every cell and atom dissolving in air.

Causa Sui

After my mother died, the truest thing
I could say was there are no words.
Yet words were all I, motherless
sack emptied of air, had, so I
used them, wielded them
with my dissociated mind
and slow bleed of a heart,
emitted from a tiny mouth,
to assure others I was alive.
It's enough that she is gone,
I thought, and I have to go on
absent my source of life and joy,
her being replaced by phantoms—
now you want me to make words,
produce language like a machine?
Horror, I spat. Gut-wrenching pain.
Where's that document I requested,
my boss had every right to demand,
and did. It's coming, I said, and in
a very real way, it's already here,
but she didn't speak that tongue.
My words, spoken to my mother,
need no translation: we were one.
My words to her were freely given,
not wrested from me as a confession
of diminished ability to serve others
or continuing incapacity to survive.
But to refuse them is to refuse her,
due acknowledgment of a debt
forgiven, never to be repaid.
No matter if I abjure fluency—
with these words I carry her,
my world, beyond the grave.

Notes

"Miraculous" references the Beatitudes (Matthew 5:4), "Blessed are those who mourn."

The lines "While the main purpose of a door / is to admit, its secondary purpose is to exclude" in "Valediction" are borrowed from Edith Wharton.

The line "You don't need metaphor to see the animal you are" in "Solar Plexus" is borrowed from Annie Goold.

The lines "O cocaine, won't you tell me, when / I wake and only my dream remains / who I am, sheared of my golden mane?" in "Ex-Voto" are reconfigured from Tiffany Troy, and the line "After the light Blake calls experience" in "Ex-Voto" is also from Tiffany Troy.

The lines "No woman needs / intercourse: few women escape it" in "Convert" are borrowed from Andrea Dworkin.

The lines "Why did I cry today for an hour, / with my whole body, the way babies cry?" in "Fin du Monde" are borrowed from Jane Kenyon.

The phrase "in that deep inaction where music reigns" in "Metaphysical" is borrowed from Yannis Ritsos, and the phrase "fixed to that chariot in war," from Rachel Hadas.

The lines "I lie horizontal and think about the rain, / how the garden has not yet been seeded" in "Childlessness" are borrowed from James Merrill.

The following lines in "Sonata" are adapted from Bruce Bond: "Every voice an epitaph, then a little tune," and "Perfection: from the Latin *perfectus*, / meaning a hollow object, complete."

The line "We have never not / been modern" in "Apocalypse" references Bruno Latour's book *We Have Never Been Modern*.

The lines "I am the place where thinking was. / I don't face the world, I face a wall" in "Human Resources" are borrowed from Brian Henry.

The line "This is my horse, abstraction" in "Sturm und Drang" is adapted from Louise Glück, as well as the line "The songs feel alien: the unspeakable entered them" in "Optimism."

The lines "If the heart is a temple, / each statue will be broken" in "Overture" reconfigures a line from Agha Shahid Ali.

The line "I will praise you, not the mutilated world" in "Requiem" reconfigures a line from Adam Zagajewski.

"Gloria Patri" is a hymn of praise in Christian liturgies. Lines 36-37 are from Psalm 91.